IMAGES
of America

AROUND HALEDON
IMMIGRATION AND LABOR

IMAGES
of America

AROUND HALEDON
IMMIGRATION AND LABOR

Angelica M. Santomauro
and Evelyn M. Hershey

ARCADIA
PUBLISHING

Published by Arcadia Publishing
Charleston SC, Chicago IL, Portsmouth NH, San Francisco CA

Library of Congress Catalog Card Number: 2007939750

For all general information contact Arcadia Publishing at:
Telephone 843-853-2070
Fax 843-853-0044
E-mail sales@arcadiapublishing.com
For customer service and orders:
Toll-Free 1-888-313-2665

Visit us on the Internet at www.arcadiapublishing.com

This book is dedicated to New Jersey's working people and immigrants who sacrificed and persevered to establish justice in the workplace as a means of paving a less challenging road on which we all walk.

CONTENTS

ACKNOWLEDGMENTS

Around Haledon: Immigration and Labor would not have been possible without the generosity of Haledon residents who donated photographs and documents to the American Labor Museum's collection. Thanks go to the museum's first executive director, John A. Herbst, who earnestly worked on gathering the collection piece by piece; museum volunteer Theresa Van Der Meer, who enthusiastically assisted with scanning images; college intern Alessandro Barchi, who helped conduct research; and the museum's board of trustees who enabled the staff to devote countless work hours on the project. Special thanks are extended to Steve Golin, author of *The Fragile Bridge: Paterson Silk Strike 1913*, who contributed significantly to the history of the labor movement. Finally the authors are deeply grateful to their families for their unwavering support and encouragement.

INTRODUCTION

During the latter 19th and early 20th centuries, many Europeans left their homelands to embark upon a new life in America; a large number of those who arrived into the Port of New York made their way across the Hudson River to settle in New Jersey. Regarded as one of the highest industrialized states in the nation, New Jersey offered employment opportunities to these newly arrived immigrants. In the northwest corner of the state, the thunderous and powerful water flowing from the Great Falls in Paterson, Passaic County, provided energy to nearly 300 silk mills in the city. Thousands of immigrant workers (men, women, and children) toiled day and night to make fine silk for the few who could afford to purchase the luxurious cloth. Many of those immigrant silk mill workers traveled by foot or trolley car from the neighboring borough of Haledon.

Haledon, originally part of Manchester Township, was once called Oldham and Deer Hill. It was one of the first communities in the country to be developed by the trolley car. As early as 1881, trolleys were running every half hour to Paterson. In 1908, when this streetcar suburb, measuring only 1.3 miles square, officially became the borough of Haledon, it housed approximately 160 families. The blending of the predominantly English, Scotch, Dutch, German, and northern Italian families allowed for a community rich in diverse cultures. One land company advertised to working families, "If you buy land in Haledon, you purchase a slice of the earth." Those who flocked to the area were looking to escape crowded city boardinghouses and apartments. Land companies promoted Haledon's pure air and water, with work sites at close proximity.

Although there were three mills in Haledon, most of the country's silk was manufactured in Paterson, also known as the "Silk City." The city, however, experienced serious labor problems for many years. In 1913, Haledon rose to prominence in American labor history when over 20,000 striking silk mill workers from Paterson exited the city and safely gathered in Haledon, holding their Industrial Workers of the World (IWW) union meetings at Haledon's Barbour Square and at the Botto House (a weaver's home) on Norwood Street. Haledon swiftly became known as a "haven for free speech."

In 1917, when the United States became involved in World War I, many of those who went to fight overseas were from Haledon. As with all wars, lives were lost, views changed, and political unrest began. The immigrant traditions remained, but many households were becoming Americanized. Haledon, which was one of only two New Jersey towns with a socialist mayor, elected a Republican Party mayoral candidate in 1920. Five years later, however, voters brought back their former mayor, who ran on a Progressive Party ticket, and faith in his leadership was restored.

By the close of the decade, many new homes had been built in Haledon. Families accumulated the latest consumer goods and services, such as vacuum cleaners, kitchen ranges, indoor plumbing, and electricity. Businesses were incorporated, religious congregations grew, newspapers were printed, and community organizations for adults and children were created. Haledon was on the map as a socially progressive community. Whether one lived in or around Haledon, it was the spot to go and recreate on a leisurely Sunday afternoon, shop on the avenue, or visit family and friends.

One

IMMIGRATION

Pietro Botto (standing center), his wife, Maria (seated, second from right), and daughter Albina (seated far right) arrived at Ellis Island in 1892. They hailed from Biella, Piedmonte, Italy, a leading textile center, and first settled in Union City, New Jersey. By 1910, the date of this photograph, the Bottos were living in their newly built home in Haledon, and the family included three more daughters, Olga (standing left), Eva (seated first left), and Adele (seated center). (Courtesy of American Labor Museum/Botto House National Landmark.)

The D'Andrea family and friends are enjoying a leisurely day together. Family was very important to the Italian immigrants. Many families looked forward to Sundays (the only day the mills closed) to have a "social life" and enjoy traditions from their homeland. Women exchanged recipes, stories, and everyday happenings. Children were permitted to "run loose" and interact with cousins and friends. The men enjoyed homemade wine, bocce, and card games. These simple pleasures made for an enjoyable day. (Courtesy of American Labor Museum/Botto House National Landmark.)

BIELLA - Entrata da Porta Torino

Biella, Italy, at the foothills of the Alps, was a leading textile producer of linen, wool, and silk. Many who had worked in Biella as weavers immigrated to the city of Paterson and the surrounding area and took up weaving. These newly arrived workers maintained ties to their hometown through letters and postcards, making it easier for others to follow. (Courtesy of American Labor Museum/Botto House National Landmark.)

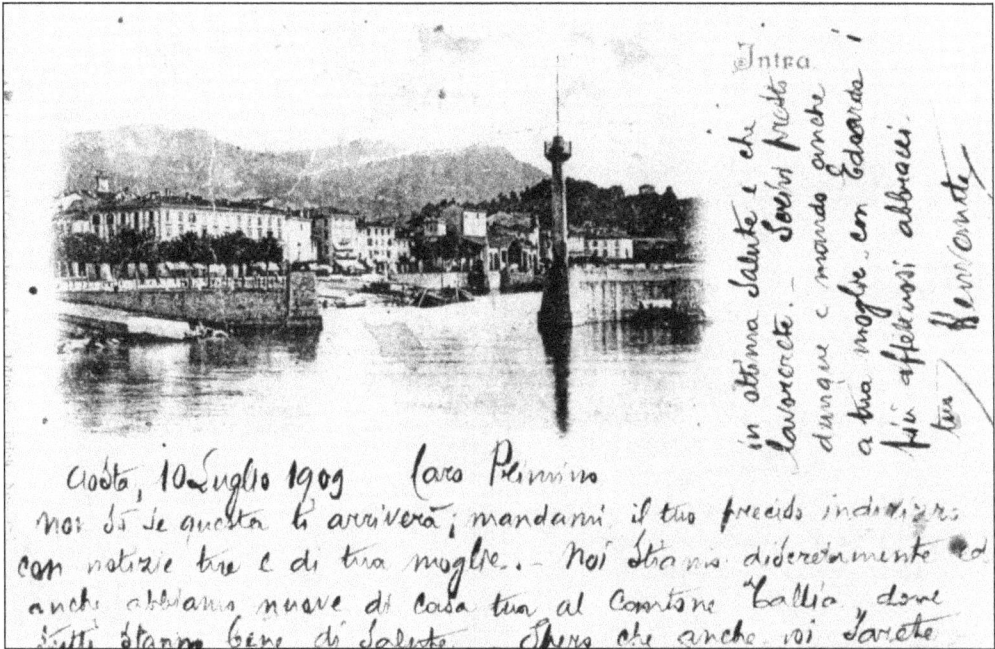

Costa, 10 Luglio 1909   Caro Primino
Noi ... se questa ti arriverà; mandami il tuo preciso indirizzi
con notizie tue e di tua moglie. — Noi Stiamo discretamente ed
anche abbiamo nuove di Casa tua al Comtone Callio dove
tutti stanno bene di Salute. Spero che anche voi Sarete
in ottima salute e che lavorerete. — Servo molto dunque e mando anche a tua moglie en Edoardo i più affetuosi abbracci. tua Benvenuto

Intra

By 1910, there were 7,000 to 8,000 Italians working in the manufacturing of silk in Paterson. Family and friends were left behind. Postcards and letters were the only means of communication between America and Italy. Both the immigrants in America and family and friends still in Italy anxiously awaited news of their loved ones. Many postcards depicted scenes of the immigrants' hometowns or formal family photographs. (Courtesy of American Labor Museum/Botto House National Landmark.)

Matilda Grande's mother proudly wears the folk costume of the Lombard region of Italy. Most likely, she made the dress herself. "Frenchy," as she was called by her boss, mill owner Catholina Lambert, was born at Lake Como and immigrated to America at the age of 10. She was employed as a domestic and errand girl by the Lambert household. (Courtesy of American Labor Museum/Botto House National Landmark.)

This is the Italian military exit visa of Alfredo Azzi, who was born in Rivarlo, Italy, in 1886 and arrived in the United States at the port of New York on December 1, 1906. Like so many immigrants from northern Italy, Azzi went to work in the silk mills as a dyer. (Courtesy of American Labor Museum/ Botto House National Landmark.)

Silk dyer Alfredo Azzi and his wife, Emma Azzi (née Gallo), are pictured beneath their grape arbor on Clinton Street, in Haledon around 1913. The couple was married in Haledon on October 26, 1912. (Courtesy of American Labor Museum/Botto House National Landmark.)

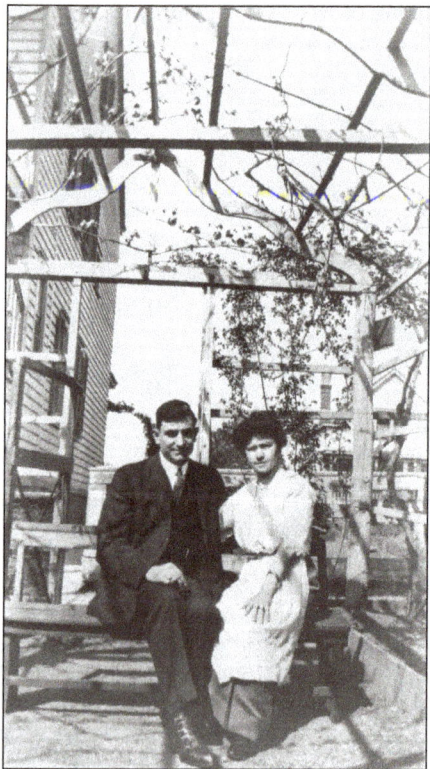

Attilio "Til" Azzi, seen here at six months, was the son of Alfredo Azzi and Emma Azzi (née Gallo) and was born in 1916. A first-generation Haledonite, Til grew up surrounded by an extended family of Azzis and Gallos. (Courtesy of American Labor Museum/ Botto House National Landmark.)

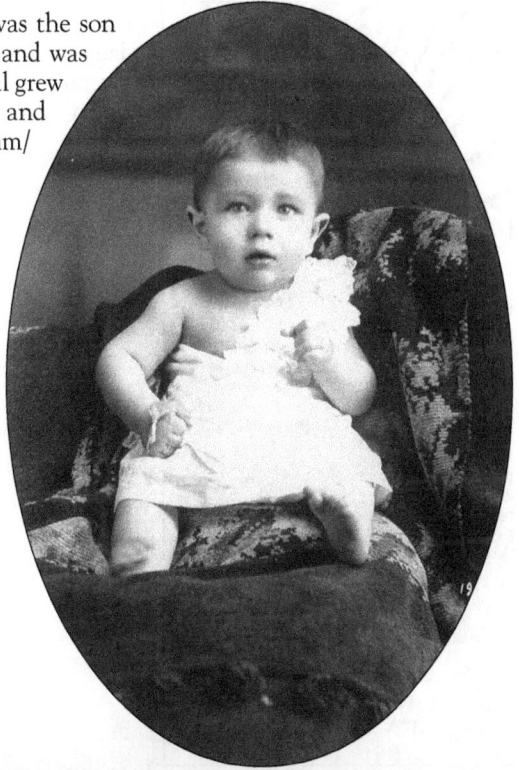

Attilio's christening in 1917 presented the occasion for this photograph of family and friends in Haledon. The boy's parents were immigrants from northern Italy. Attilio's father worked in dye shops that served the local silk industry. The Azzi, Botto Coda, and Frignoca families were part of the growing Piedmontese community of Haledon in the late 19th and early 20th centuries. (Courtesy of American Labor Museum/Botto House National Landmark.)

Emma Azzi (née Gallo) is babysitting Dorothy Rolleri, daughter of Louis and Cora Rolleri, at their home on Katz Avenue, Haledon. (Courtesy of American Labor Museum/Botto House National Landmark.)

Pictured at their home on West Clinton Street in Haledon are Attilio Azzi's maternal grandparents, Emilio and Maria Gallo. (Courtesy of American Labor Museum/Botto House National Landmark.)

Ernest Roffino (standing, far left), a mason and contractor, poses for a photograph with family and friends on Burhans Avenue in Haledon in 1923. (Courtesy of Doris Roffino Ververs and Edward J. Torasso.)

The Azzi-Gallo family enjoys a Sunday picnic at the Haledon Spring, 1919. (Courtesy of American Labor Museum/Botto House National Landmark.)

At the Robatino home at 315 West Clinton Street in Haledon, Henrietta Van De Voort (center) talks over the fence with Brigida Robatino (left) and Eva Allaghi (right) with Irving Allaghi in her arms. Darwin Van De Voort stands in the foreground. These Haledon residents were photographed in 1924. (Courtesy of Laura Van De Voort Allaghi.)

Darwin poses for a snapshot from a garden of his family's home at 315 West Clinton Street in Haledon. A clothesline can be seen strung above his head. Behind the fence is Cook Street. (Courtesy of Laura Van De Voort Allaghi.)

Laura Van De Voort and Mary Tetamenti bathe near Belmont Avenue in Haledon around 1930. The brook emptied into a lake in Lakeside Park along Haledon Avenue. (Courtesy of Laura Van De Voort Allaghi.)

"Grandpa" Guido Robatino and grandson Darwin sit for a photograph at the Van De Voort home, 315 West Clinton Street, Haledon in 1924. (Courtesy of Laura Van De Voort Allaghi.)

Haledon resident Ernest Roffino sits at the steering wheel of his commercial vehicle, which is parked in front of the home of Lorenzo and Elisa Gremmo, located at 174 Lily Street in Paterson. The Gremmos and other family and friends assemble behind the truck for this photograph taken in the early 1920s. (Courtesy of Doris Roffino Ververs and Edward J. Torasso.)

Ernest Roffino (right) is working on the construction of a home, probably in Haledon, during the early 1920s. Homes built by this mason and contractor include his home at 207 Burhans Avenue. (Courtesy of Doris Roffino Ververs.)

Ernest Roffino, his wife, Severina, and their sons, Aldo (left), age eight years, and Louis (right), age 10 years, sailed from Genoa, Italy, and arrived at Ellis Island on October 9, 1920. The family settled in Haledon and suffered the loss of Aldo, age nine, to diphtheria on November 29, 1920. (Courtesy of Doris Roffino Ververs.)

Louis Roffino (second from right), age 14 years, and other violin students gather around their teacher for a photograph taken in Haledon in 1924. (Courtesy of Doris Roffino Ververs.)

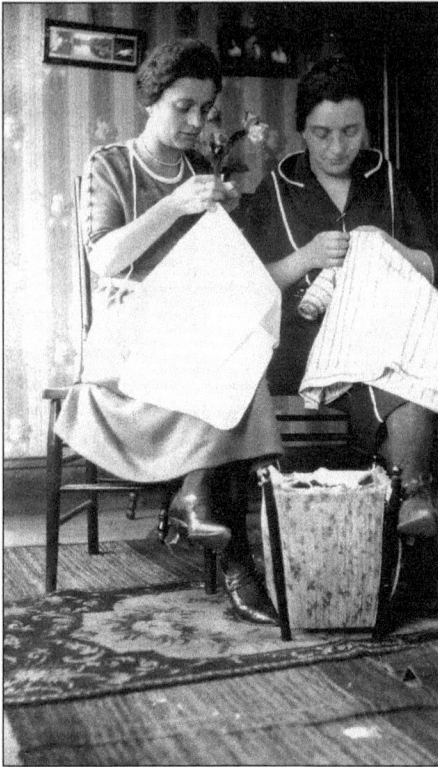

In the home of Joseph and Maria Torasso, located at 219 Burhans Avenue in Haledon, Severina Roffino (left) and Maria Torasso (right) are working on linens. Tatting, crochet, and other forms of needlework were used to create household linens. (Courtesy of Doris Roffino Ververs.)

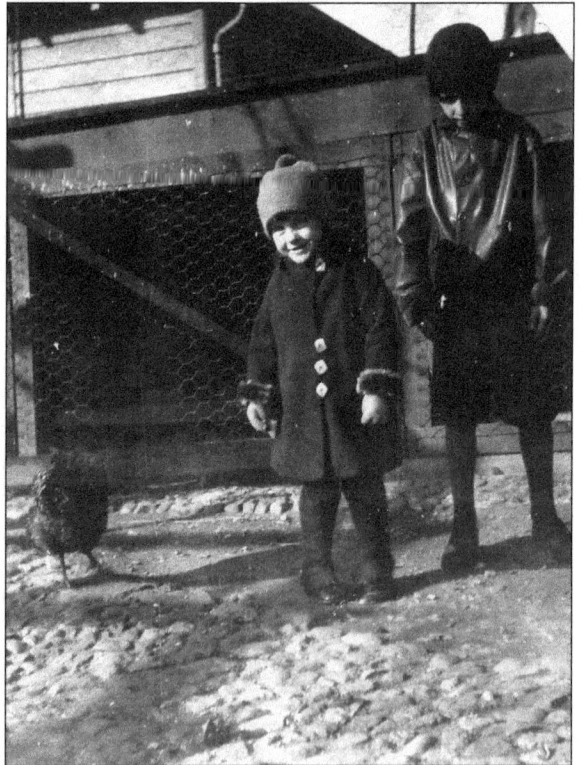

Laura Van De Voort (left), age four years, and Darwin Van De Voort (right), age nine years, stand with a family chicken at their grandparents' home, 315 West Clinton Street in Haledon. When the photograph was taken, Darwin was recovering from scarlet fever. (Courtesy of Laura Van De Voort Allaghi.)

Young Louis Roffino of Haledon (center) poses for a photograph with his uncle and aunt, Giovanni Villa (far left) and Margharita Villa (second from left), cousins Luigi and Aida Villa (far right), and his parents, Ernest Roffino and Severina Roffino (rear center). (Courtesy of Doris Roffino Ververs and Edward J. Torasso.)

Louis prepares for a Sunday drive at 207 Burhans Avenue, Haledon, on August 11, 1929. (Courtesy of Doris Roffino Ververs.)

Times turned bad in Germany in the early 1890s, and life grew difficult even for weavers in plush. Young men were being forced into the army. Hoping for a better life, families and young men left the Rhineland for America. Weavers were more fortunate and were able to find jobs in the mills. (Courtesy of American Labor Museum/Botto House National Landmark.)

Seen here are scenes of communities depicted on postcards that were received by immigrants from family and friends back in the old country. (Courtesy of American Labor Museum/Botto House National Landmark.)

Textile workers of Elberfeld, Germany, joined the waves of foreign workers who found employment in the silk industry of northern New Jersey. In Europe, many had worked independently in their homes or in small workshops of master weavers. In northern New Jersey neighborhoods of Paterson and Haledon, they owned their own homes and expected to be treated as artisans. (Courtesy of American Labor Museum/ Botto House National Landmark.)

Elberfeld and Krefeld, near the Rhine River in Germany, were silk centers from which weavers and other skilled silk artisans immigrated to Paterson. This young immigrant and others, like Katherine Brueckmann (née Ruhren), wife of Haledon's Mayor William Brueckmann and a skilled weaver in Germany, for example, found work in the silk mill in the Riverside section of Paterson. (Courtesy of American Labor Museum/ Botto House National Landmark.)

Comune di _Pollone_ ⚜ STATO CIVILE

CERTIFICATO DI NASCITA

Il Sottoscritto Ufficiale dello Stato Civile certifica che dai registri per gli atti di Nascita dell'anno _1915_ esistenti in questo Comune al N. _5 parte 2 Serie B_ risulta che _Dazza Francesco_

figlio di _Angelo_

e di _Barbara Stratta_

è nato _nella Città di Paterson, contea di Passaic, Stato del New Jersey il 12 gennaio 1897_

Rilasciato il presente su carta libera a mente della legge sul bollo dovendo servire esclusivamente per ~~l'ammissione~~ _per ottenere la fedina penale e per recarsi il titolare all'Estero in carta libera_

Pollone, addì _10 Dicembre_ 192_9_

L'Ufficiale dello Stato Civile

Ernesto Andreis

This Italian document, certified in 1929, validates that Francesco Dazza was born in "the noble city of Paterson" on January 12, 1897, and is exempt from service in the Italian military. (Courtesy of American Labor Museum/Botto House National Landmark.)

Immigrant families frequented Market Street in Paterson, not far from their workplaces, for the purpose of patronizing retail businesses, banks, and services like photograph studios. (Courtesy of Paterson Museum.)

The Paterson Directory of 1913 lists newspapers that served the large Dutch community. (Courtesy of American Labor Museum/Botto House National Landmark.)

Dutch immigrants made weekly payments to the Dutch Burial Fund. Upon their death, the fund insured monies to cover the cost of the funeral to the beneficiary. (Courtesy of American Labor Museum/Botto House National Landmark.)

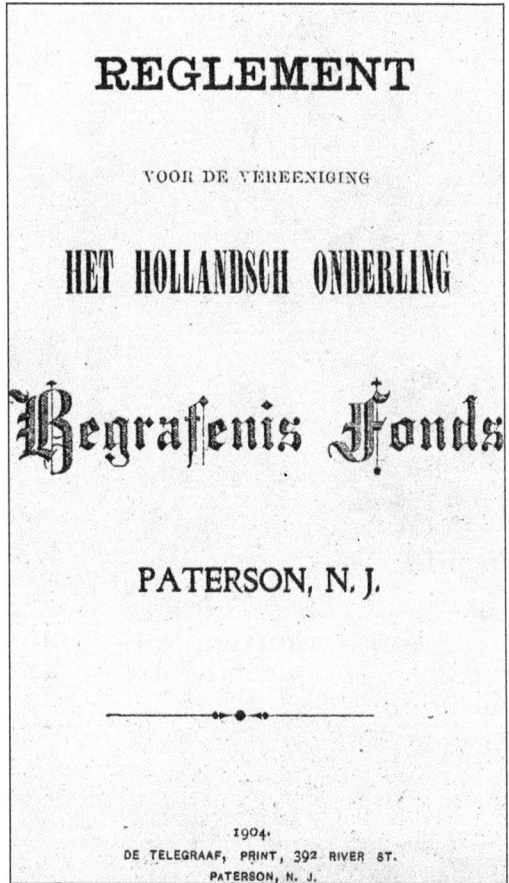

REGLEMENT

VOOR DE VEREENIGING

HET HOLLANDSCH ONDERLING

Begrafenis Fonds

PATERSON, N. J.

1904.
DE TELEGRAAF, PRINT, 392 RIVER ST.
PATERSON, N. J.

REYNOLD W. SCHREUDER, Editor.   CORNELIUS POELSTRA. Bus's Man'r.

"De Telegraaf,"
Holland   Weekly   Newspaper,

PUBLISHED AT PATERSON, N. J.

SCHREUDER & POELSTRA, Publishers.

Office : 384 and 386 River Street,
    Opp. Erie R. R. Station.   Telephone 51.

THE MARIGOLD PRINTING CO., BOOK, CATALOGUE & PRICE LISTS BRIDGEPORT, CONN.

De Telegraaf was one of the newspapers of the Dutch community. (Courtesy of American Labor Museum/Botto House National Landmark.)

Men without families and unrelated single men and women routinely found lodging in households that welcomed boarders. (Courtesy of American Labor Museum/Botto House National Landmark.)

Un saluto da Strona.

This is a postcard from Strona, Italy, sent by returning immigrants to family in the Haledon area. (Courtesy of American Labor Museum/Botto House National Landmark.)

Corso Cooperativa di STRONA

This view of the Piedmontese district of Strona is featured on one of many postcards sent by Europeans in the early 20th century to immigrants residing in and around Haledon. (Courtesy of American Labor Museum/Botto House National Landmark.)

The Guabello family reunion in 1921 included members in diverse professions, including silk workers, contractors, and saloonkeepers. Immigrant couples welcomed children who were first-generation Americans, and such reunions encouraged them to embrace their heritage. (Courtesy of American Labor Museum/Botto House National Landmark.)

29

A stereopticon card presents a view of the crowded deck of the *Konigin Luise*, a steamship leaving the German port of Bremen with immigrants bound for New York City in 1901. Steerage passage across the Atlantic Ocean cost between $20 and $30. Upon arriving in New York City, many immigrants settled in Paterson and Haledon to work in the mills. (Courtesy of Paterson Museum.)

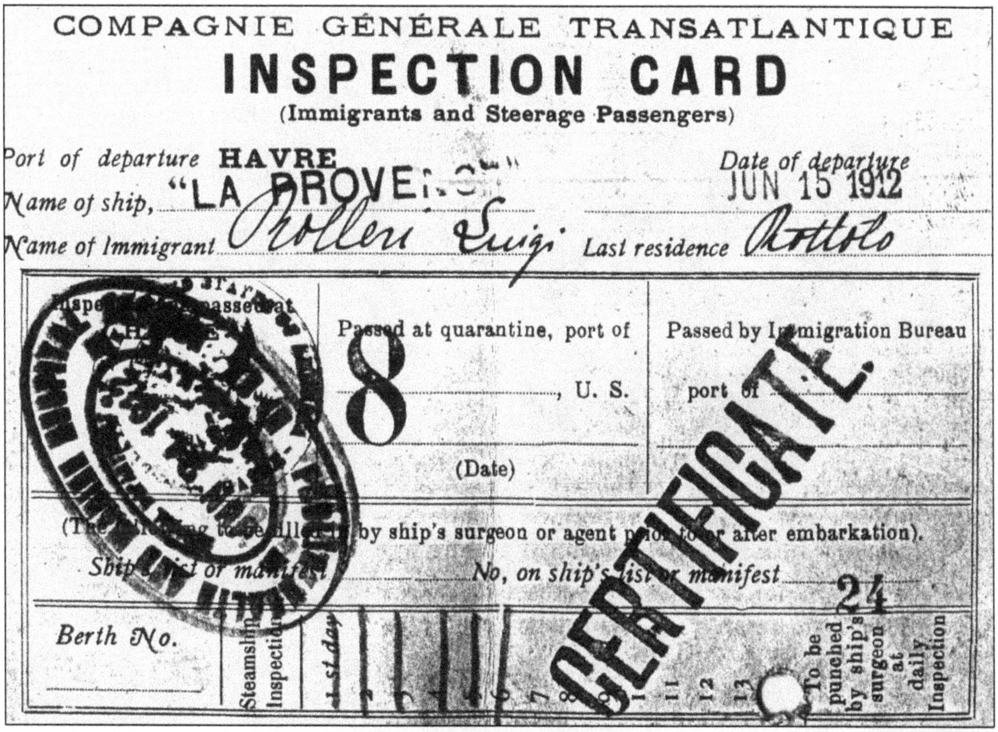

COMPAGNIE GÉNÉRALE TRANSATLANTIQUE

INSPECTION CARD

(Immigrants and Steerage Passengers)

Port of departure HAVRE *Date of departure* JUN 15 1912

Name of ship, "LA PROVENCE"

Name of Immigrant Rolleri Luigi *Last residence* Rottolo

Passed at quarantine, port of ..., U. S. 8 (Date)

Passed by Immigration Bureau port of

CERTIFICATE

(The following to be filled in by ship's surgeon or agent prior to or after embarkation).

Ship's list or manifest ... *No, on ship's list or manifest* 24

Berth No. ... Steamship Inspection ... 1st day 2 3 4 5 6 7 8 9 10 11 12 13 ... To be punched by ship's surgeon at daily Inspection

This card was pinned to the collar of Luigi Rolleri by a debarkation ships officer. This avoided any detention examination or interview by the Ellis Island quarantine officers. Rolleri settled in Haledon. (Courtesy of American Labor Museum/Botto House National Landmark.)

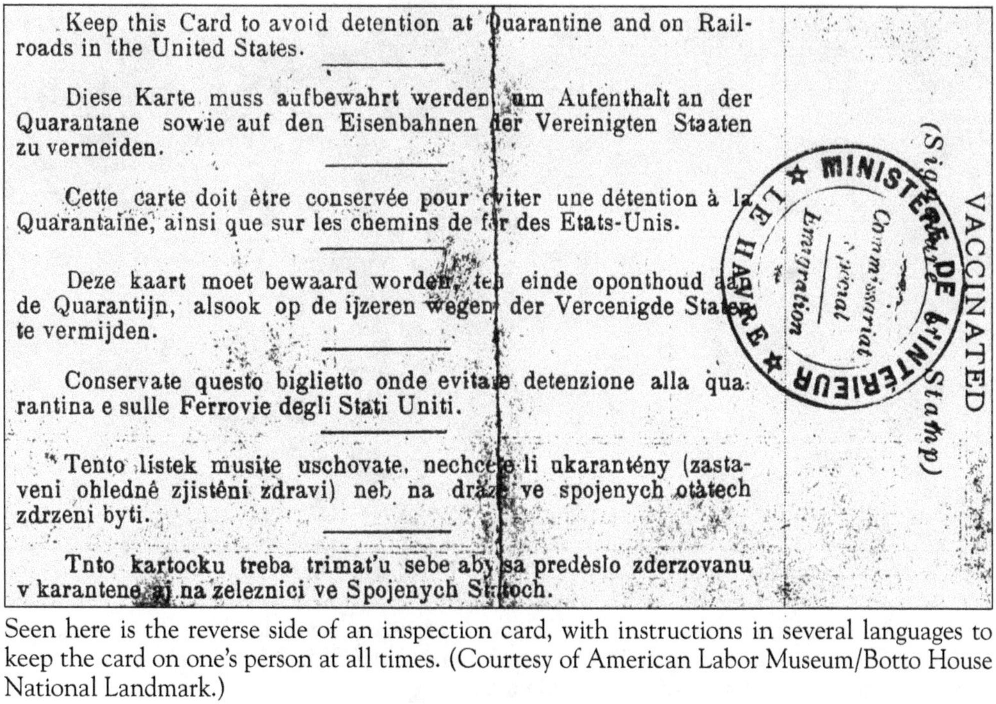

Keep this Card to avoid detention at Quarantine and on Railroads in the United States.

Diese Karte muss aufbewahrt werden um Aufenthalt an der Quarantane sowie auf den Eisenbahnen der Vereinigten Staaten zu vermeiden.

Cette carte doit être conservée pour éviter une détention à la Quarantaine, ainsi que sur les chemins de fer des Etats-Unis.

Deze kaart moet bewaard worden, ten einde oponthoud aan de Quarantijn, alsook op de ijzeren wegen der Vercenigde Staten te vermijden.

Conservate questo biglietto onde evitare detenzione alla quarantina e sulle Ferrovie degli Stati Uniti.

Tento lístek musite uschovate, nechcete li ukarantény (zastaveni ohledné zjistêni zdravi) neb na dráze ve spojenych otàtech zdrzeni byti.

Tnto kartocku treba trimat'u sebe aby sa predèslo zderzovanu v karantene aj na zeleznici ve Spojenych Statoch.

Seen here is the reverse side of an inspection card, with instructions in several languages to keep the card on one's person at all times. (Courtesy of American Labor Museum/Botto House National Landmark.)

Maria Boggio Botto (standing right) was photographed with female relatives in Biella, Italy, before immigrating to America with her husband, Pietro. Maria was a skilled silk mill worker who did piecework in her Haledon home. (Courtesy of American Labor Museum/Botto House National Landmark.)

This military discharge, dated 1887, released Pietro Botto, age 23, from a six-year tour of service in the Italian army. Fearing a second draft in 1892, Pietro, his wife, Maria, and their young daughter Albina immigrated to the United States from Biella, Piedmont, Italy. They eventually built their home in Haledon, where Pietro worked in the Cedar Cliff Mill. (Courtesy of American Labor Museum/Botto House National Landmark.)

Pietro and Maria Botto and their daughter Albina (standing) pose for a photograph taken at the birth of the Bottos' daughter Adelia in 1894. Pietro Botto, a skilled weaver who also painted church interiors in Italy, easily found textile work in northern New Jersey. Between 1892 and 1908, the Bottos lived in West Hoboken (today's Union City) New Jersey. (Courtesy of American Labor Museum/ Botto House National Landmark.)

In this image, Italians offer a toast to the "salame," a tasty northern Italian sausage that they have made at home in Haledon with a meat grinder, a scale, and ingredients from local merchants. (Courtesy of American Labor Museum/Botto House National Landmark.)

Getuigschrift van verandering van werkelijke woonplaats.   Nummer

Door de volgende personen is, overeenkomstig art. 14 van 's Konings Besluit van 27 Juli 1887, (Staatsblad No. 140), verklaart, dat deze metterwoon verlaten, om zich te vestigen in de Gemeente _Lodi. N. Noord Amerika._

FAMILIENAAM. (Familienaam der vrouw.)	VOORNAMEN. (Voluit geschreven.)	Geslacht (Mannelijk.) (Vrouwelijk.) M. V.	Betrekking tot het hoofd van het huisgezin.	Dagteekening en Jaar van Geboorte.	GEBOORTEPLAATS. (Met aanwijzing der Provincie voor Inboorlingen, van het land voor vreemdelingen.)	Burgerl. Staat. O.H.W.S.	KERKGE- NOOTSCHAP. (Elk bepaald op te geven.)	AMBT, BEROEP of BEDRIJF. Bij bedrijven vermelden of men hoofd (H) is of onder- geschikte (O).	Opgave omtrent het wettig domicilie.	Aanme
Rij van	× Cornelis Johannus	M	Hoofd	10 Jan 1869	Brielle	H	N.H.	Schipper H	—	
Waspolder	Flora Hendrika	V	Vrouw	17 Jan 1869	Brielle	H	N.H.	—		
Rij van	× Joseph	M	Zoon	... 1893	Brielle	O	N.H.	—		
Rij van	Wilhelmina	V	Dochter	18 Mei 1896	Brielle	O	N.H.	—		
Rij van	Cornelis Johannes	M	Zoon	18 Mei 1901	Brielle	O	N.H.	—		

Handteekening van den belanghebbende,

Afgegeven door het Bestuur der Gemeente BRIE
BRIELLE, den _20 Juni_ 191

De Secretaris,   De Burgeme
LAURENSE.   N. J. C. S. H.

This document was issued to immigrants leaving Brielle, Holland, in 1911, listing name, birth date, and relationship to head of family. (Courtesy of Van Der Meer family.)

Many Dutch immigrants owned boats in Holland. Some families lived onboard. (Courtesy of Van Der Meer family.)

Pictured here is a Dutch couple in typical Dutch apparel. (Courtesy of Van Der Meer family.)

Two

EMPLOYMENT AND
WORKPLACES

Here is a portrait of workers (men and boys) before the Rogers Locomotive Company, which was the largest of three locomotive plants in Paterson in the late 19th century. The company produced 10–12 engines a month during the Civil War. It continued operating until 1926. (Courtesy of Paterson Museum.)

Haledon is approximately one mile from the Great Falls National Landmark in Paterson. The water drops 77 feet, and it is the second-largest waterfall in volume east of the Mississippi, after Niagara Falls. It is connected to a unique three-tiered waterpower system, which produced energy for area mills. (Courtesy of American Labor Museum/Botto House National Landmark.)

Photographed here is the Society of Established Useful Manufacturers (SUM) hydroelectric plant and the Great Falls (right) around 1916. The SUM was established to assist in the development of an industrial city. The plant was used to generate electricity for many factories in the area. (Courtesy of Paterson Museum.)

Paterson was a transportation and business hub. Many retail stores and banks lined Main Street. Trolley cars were a popular means of public transportation, connecting Paterson to Haledon and other neighboring streetcar suburbs. Walking to downtown Paterson on Sundays to window shop was a relaxing and common pastime. (Courtesy of American Labor Museum/Botto House National Landmark.)

Family-owned grocery stores were common. The Van Riper business of Paterson sold fresh fruit and vegetables in horse-drawn carriages by going up and down local streets. (Courtesy of Paterson Museum.)

Dyeing gave silk the lustrous colors that attracted the consumer. Many master dyers who came to America were from Lyons, France, and the Lombardy region of Italy. Silk dyeing was a modern chemical industry. Dyers and master dyers, considered skilled employees, were paid competitive wages. (Courtesy of American Labor Museum/ Botto House National Landmark.)

C. DE GRADO SILK DYEING CO., INC.

The C. De Grado Silk Dyeing Company was incorporated in 1916 by Costabele De Grado, a native of Salerno, Italy. By 1920, when a new mill was completed, the company employed over 100 people. (Courtesy of American Labor Museum/Botto House National Landmark.)

The high-quality goods of Paterson silk manufacturers depended upon the skills and artisan pride of silk workers of Haledon and other neighboring communities. (Courtesy of American Labor Museum/Botto House National Landmark.)

THE AMERICAN SILK JOURNAL.   iii

WILLIAM ✴ RYLE ✴ & ✴ CO.,

DOMESTIC   IMPORTERS OF   DEALERS IN

THROWN SILK   ASIATIC AND EUROPEAN   Foreign

Of all Descriptions,   **RAW SILK,**   AND

ON HAND OR TO ORDER.   Domestic

Fine Pure Dye Silks for the Wool-   54 HOWARD STREET,   Spun Silk Yarns

len Trade a Specialty.   *NEW YORK.*   AND NOILS.

THE NATCHAUG SILK CO.,

WILLIMANTIC, CONN.,

MANUFACTURERS OF

DRESS ✴ SILKS, ✴ SERGES, ✴ AND ✴ SATINS,

SILK AND MOHAIR BRAIDS,

SEWING SILKS AND TWISTS.

NEW YORK   CHICAGO

OFFICE AND SALESROOMS: ✴   OFFICE AND SALESROOMS:

No. 546 Broadway.   Nos. 213 & 215 Fifth Ave.

Telephone, No. 198

FREDERIC HAND & CO.,

Jacquard ⁙ Designers,

157 Van Houten Street, Paterson, N. J.

HESS, ✚ GOLDSMITH ✚ & ✚ CO.

MANUFACTURERS OF **SILK GOODS:**

HIGH NOVELTIES,   — PLAIN GOODS,—   CREPE DE CHINE

Mills: { Paterson, New Jersey.   — Salesroom: —

{ Wilkes Barre, Pennsylvania.   No. 89 GRAND STREET, NEW YORK.

The dye house workers, who were responsible for dipping skeins of silk into vats of boiling water and acids, were largely unskilled workers from the agricultural regions of southern Italy, the Netherlands, and the Middle East. Their working conditions were the worst in the silk industry. Dye houses were filled with steam and fumes. In the summer, the steam was suffocating, and in the winter, the steam would condense and even freeze. A worker in 1913 declared, "the dye house is the most dirty and unhealthy part of the silk industry." (Courtesy of American Labor Museum/Botto House National Landmark.)

John Ryle is known as "the father of the American silk industry." He was an experienced weaver in his native Macclesfield, England, and came to the United States in 1839. Ryle was the first in this country to put silk on a spool. The successful experiment was a result of a conference with Elias Howe, inventor of the Howe sewing machine. This was the beginning of the spool silk industry in this country. (Courtesy of Paterson Museum.)

Yours truly
Benjamin B. Tilt

Benjamin B. Tilt came to this country from Coventry, England, at the age of 28, with the belief that in America, his skills as a silk worker would make him successful. He first went to Philadelphia, where the silk industry was still in its infancy, but was unable to secure work. He became discouraged and went to New York City, only to find the same situation. He finally found work with McCrary Silk Manufacturers. His ambitious spirit led to many business dealings. In 1855, he came to Paterson and organized the Phoenix Silk Manufacturing Company, which grew to be one of the largest silk mills in the Paterson area. (Courtesy of American Labor Museum/Botto House National Landmark.)

Robert Hamil, an early silk entrepreneur, was pioneer of the jacquard weaving process. (Courtesy of Paterson Museum.)

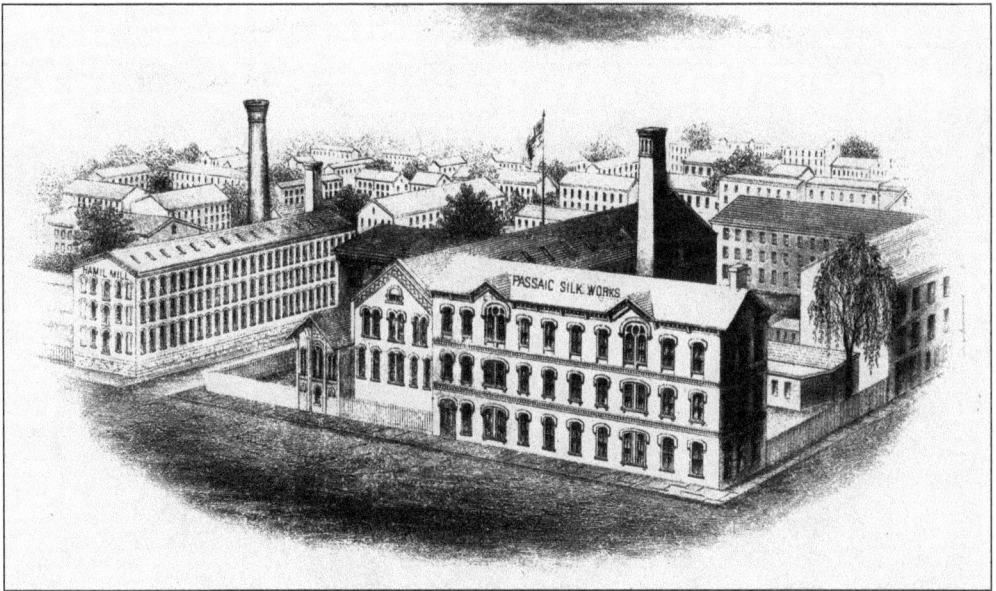

Robert Hamil and James Booth entered into a copartnership and started a business in 1855. They commenced in a small way in the Beaver Mill during the infant silk enterprises of the period. They put in machinery and began with 20 operatives who worked as "throwsters." After 15 years, they gradually went into the production of grosgrain ribbons, fringed silks, silk handkerchiefs, scarves, millinery silks, and other silk products. They went on to have one of the most successful businesses in Paterson, where many Haledon residents were employed. (Courtesy of Paterson Museum.)

Many silk manufacturers had begun running branches in Pennsylvania to avoid labor disputes and take advantage of cheaper labor of women and children of coal miners. Advertisements in the Paterson Directory of 1912–1913 informed potential customers of businesses' multiple locations. (Courtesy of American Labor Museum/Botto House National Landmark.)

Male workers of the Helvetia Silk Company socialize during an outing. The work rules and loud machinery at the mills allowed for little, if any, opportunity to converse with one another. (Courtesy of American Labor Museum/Botto House National Landmark.)

Many English silk weavers, seeking better employment opportunities, came to Haledon and Paterson in the late 1880s, when the silk industry was booming. Among the occupations of the silk industry, weavers were highly respected for their skill in operating the complex power looms. (Courtesy of American Labor Museum/Botto House National Landmark.)

This group of Dutch American silk mill workers poses for a photograph in 1894. Laborers who were descendants of earlier immigrants from England, Ireland, France, Holland, and Germany were joined in the factories in the late 19th and early 20th centuries by large numbers of new immigrants hailing from Italy, Poland, Russia, Syria, and Armenia. (Courtesy of American Labor Museum/Botto House National Landmark.)

New immigrants to America needed not only to locate a job but housing was needed as well. Ethnic neighborhoods developed. Milan Flats, pictured here, provided housing in close proximity to the mills. Such boardinghouses helped to alleviate crowding and fulfilled the need to be with those from one's homeland. (Courtesy of Paterson Museum.)

BOARDING.

BOARDING.

A young man wishing good board in a private family can be accommodated at 375 Straight street.   28mar 3t

BOARDING.

Respectable gentlemen boarders can secure rooms and board at No. 14 Hotel street.   20m 9f

BOARDING.

Best home in Paterson for respectable boarders is at 14 HOTEL STREET.   24mar 1mo

BOARDING.

A few gentlemen can be accommodated with board in a private family. Rooms all warm and comfortable. Call at 153 Ward street, near Prince street.   Feb 14-42t

Furnished Rooms to Rent.

Very desirable furnished rooms with all modern conveniences.   144 Broadway, between Church and Paterson streets.   21mar tf

BOARDING.

Roberts House, 201 Market street. Nicely furnished rooms with or without board. Also table board.   feb4 t

WILLIAM H SPEAD

To help supplement their income, many families took in boarders, as seen in an excerpt from the classifieds of a Paterson newspaper. Immigrants were able to have a clean bed, hot meal, and companionship in a strange land. They tried to locate a room in close proximity to the mill where they worked. (Courtesy of Paterson Museum.)

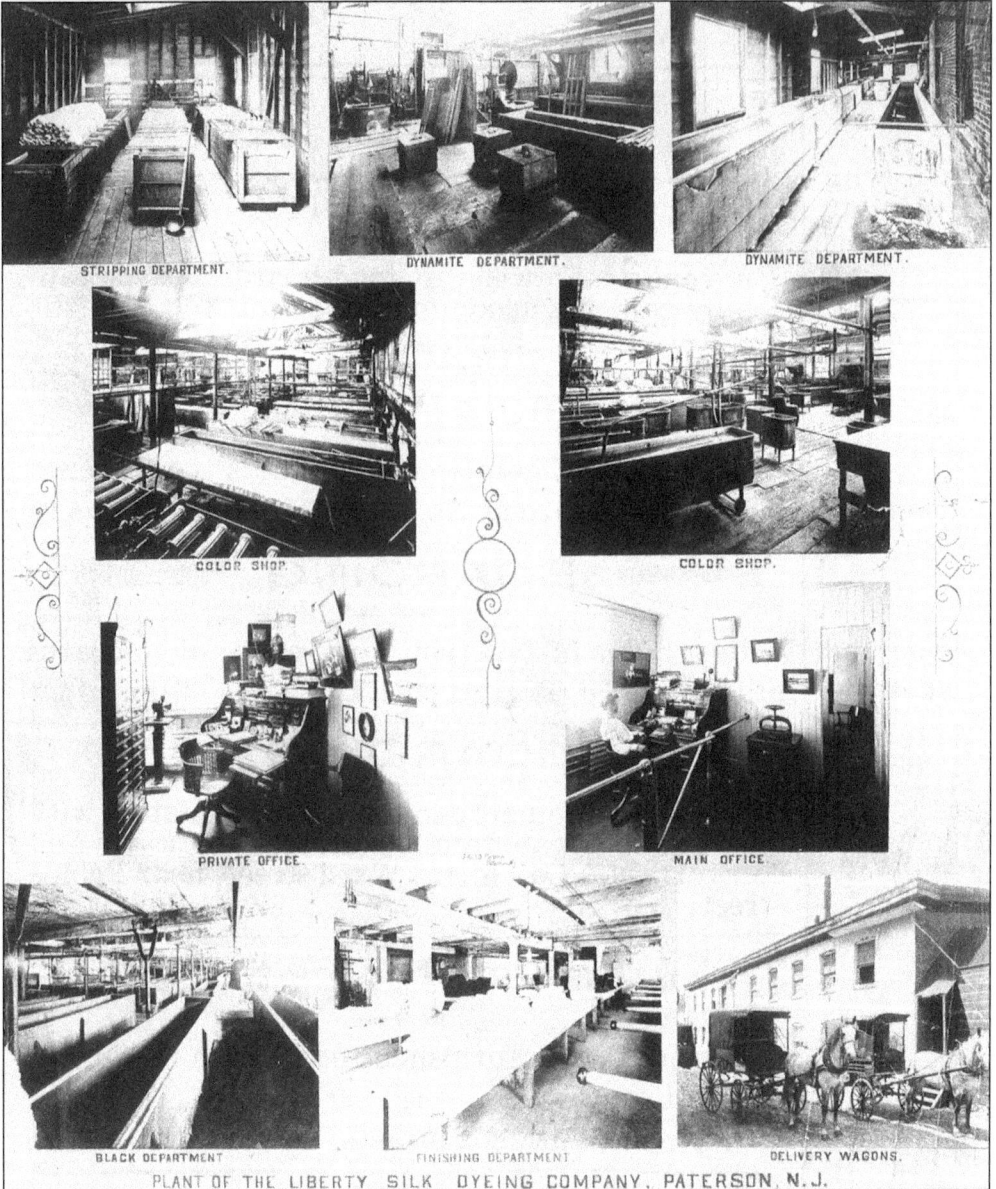

STRIPPING DEPARTMENT.

DYNAMITE DEPARTMENT.

DYNAMITE DEPARTMENT.

COLOR SHOP.

COLOR SHOP.

PRIVATE OFFICE.

MAIN OFFICE.

BLACK DEPARTMENT

FINISHING DEPARTMENT

DELIVERY WAGONS.

PLANT OF THE LIBERTY SILK DYEING COMPANY, PATERSON, N.J.

The Liberty Silk Dyeing Company of Paterson received raw silk from Italy and Asia. Thousands of pounds of silk were dyed yearly and were shipped to weaving plants. (Courtesy of American Labor Museum/Botto House National Landmark.)

These women work under the watchful eye of a supervisor. They toiled long hours without stopping until the whistle blew. "Picking," the labor undertaken here, is the inspection of woven silk and removal of knots and loose ends with a tweezerlike tool. This tedious job was also completed at home by women as piecework. Many women who stayed at home sought to contribute to the family income in this manner. (Courtesy of American Labor Museum/Botto House National Landmark.)

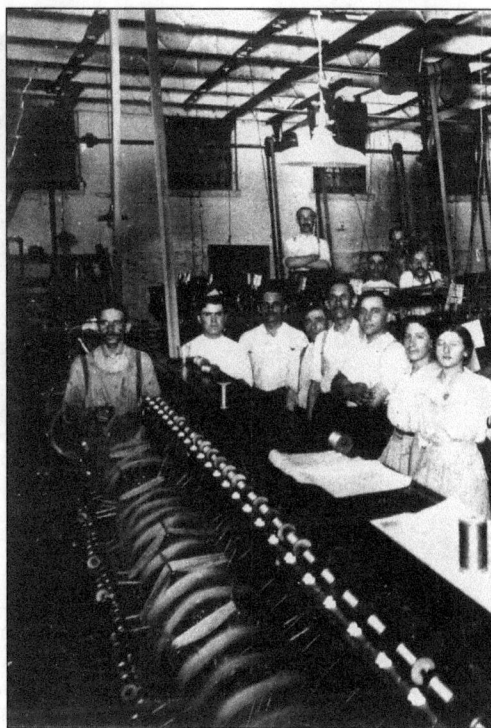

Bobbin girls (far right) in 1910 tend machinery that transfers skeins of silk to bobbins for weaving. Dust, oil, and unsanitary conditions created dangerous, even deadly hazards in the mills. Youths were especially vulnerable members of the labor force. (Courtesy of American Labor Museum/Botto House National Landmark.)

The Danforth Locomotive Machine Company and other machine shops competed in the production of the latest and most efficient silk-making equipment. Here, in a publication geared for manufacturers, Danforth Locomotive Machine Company of Paterson advertises its newest silk reel mill and spinning frame. (Courtesy of Paterson Museum.)

50

One of Haledon's three silk mills was the Cedar Cliff Mill, which offered ample employment opportunities for residents of Haledon and the surrounding area. (Courtesy of American Labor Museum/Botto House National Landmark.)

Jacquard card cutting was tedious work. Each card required a unique pattern of holes to produce the correct design pattern for the silk. If a card was not properly "cut," the loom could become inoperable. (Courtesy of Paterson Museum.)

Clara Platz was a weaver from the silk textile center in Krefeld, Germany. The workforce of the silk mills was made up of a diverse population who spoke different languages but shared knowledge of the textile industry and experience acting collectively with coworkers to improve working conditions. (Courtesy of American Labor Museum/Botto House National Landmark.)

Warpers were among the most highly skilled and paid silk workers in the early 20th century, sometimes earning $18 per week. Both men and women completed the work of setting up the warp threads on looms for the weavers. (Courtesy of Paterson Museum.)

The warp is made by winding threads from many bobbins onto a roller or beam, seen here. The finished warp is inspected by a warp picker, who snips any knotted ends from the warp. (Courtesy of Paterson Museum.)

Jacquard looms produced patterned silk for neckties and other uses in great quantity in and around Paterson. The pattern woven by each loom was dictated by the jacquard cards, punch cards, that were attached to the loom. (Courtesy of American Labor Museum/Botto House National Landmark.)

The Johnson Cowdin Mill was a ribbon mill in the city of Paterson. This ribbon mill employed many immigrant workers who resided in Haledon. (Courtesy of American Labor Museum/Botto House National Landmark.)

Often silk mills sponsored an annual workers' outing as a means of extending a paternal thank-you to employees and of boosting company morale. Many of these picnics were held in Haledon, which was a popular recreation destination for silk mill workers. (Courtesy of American Labor Museum/Botto House National Landmark.)

This advertisement from the *c.* 1893 Paterson City Business Directory reflects the complexity of the looms, which were built by machine shops located in the city. (Courtesy of Paterson Museum.)

Many fathers took their children to the mill at an early age to introduce them to the workings of the machines. They helped their fathers and, at the same time, learned a trade. A large number of children began as young as eight years of age and never left, leaving no opportunity for formal education. (Courtesy of American Labor Museum/Botto House National Landmark.)

Smokestacks and mills of Paterson appear before Garret Mountain in this view. (Courtesy of Paterson Museum.)

The industrial area of the city of Paterson, located near the Great Falls, had 298 silk mills. Plumes of exhaust from the smokestacks could be seen for miles. As one walked the streets, the smell of the textile mills was quite evident. (Courtesy of American Labor Museum/Botto House National Landmark.)

Immigrant workers with no specialized skills could find work in the silk mills. Because of the value of the silk being produced, silk mills were generally cleaner and better lit than other textile mills. (Courtesy of American Labor Museum/Botto House National Landmark.)

Alexander Zukowski was a skilled weaver from Poland. The silk mills needed skilled workers to teach those who were new to the industry. These skilled workers from Poland, France, England, and Italy were in demand and easily found employment in the mills. (Courtesy of American Labor Museum/Botto House National Landmark.)

There were many women who worked in the silk industry. At times, they were preferred because they were considered neater and cleaner in their work and at their workstations. Skirts and long hair, however, proved hazardous next to some of the machinery. (Courtesy of American Labor Museum/Botto House National Landmark.)

Men and boys worked together at various jobs in the mills. Time cards were used to verify the hours worked. Children earned less than the men but worked the same 55-hour workweek in the early 1900s. (Courtesy of American Labor Museum/Botto House National Landmark.)

Tram spinners .... 3.50 to 4.50
Organ flyer hands .... 2.75 to 4.00
Spinners .... 2.50 to 3.50
Reelers .... 3.00 to 3.50
Lacers .... 1.25 to 2.50
Bobbin boys .... 2.50 to 3.25

This illustrates very well the difficulty of the competition referred to, if these figures are correct.

The arbitrator decided that the mills which were parties to the arbitration should reduce their working hours to 55 per week, and should adopt the following minimum wage scale for throwing mills:

Rates Fixed by the Arbitrator.
WAGES TO BE PAID IN THROWING DEPARTMENT.

Minimum rate for winders, doublers and twisters (second time spinners):

Per week.

Learners up to six months $2.00
After six months, to twelve months 2.50
After twelve months to eighteen months 3.00
After eighteen months to twenty-four months 3.75
After twenty-four months, at least 4.50
Tussah workers, 50 cts. per week additional, or .. 5.00

Minimum rate for first time spinners and reelers:

Learners up to six months $2.00
After six months to twelve months 2.50
After twelve months to eighteen months 3.00
After eighteen months to twenty-four months 3.50
After twenty-four months, at least 4.00

(NOTE.—At this writing—March, 1913—a general advance in wages of 10% has been granted in most of the throwing mills in Eastern Pennsylvania.)

In this connection, some figures published in 1910 by the U. S. Government, shewing wages paid in the silk industry abroad, as compared with the average wages paid here, may be of interest.

WAGES IN THE SILK TRADE.

A comparison of wages in the United States and foreign countries is as follows:

Data gathered by the federal government in 1911 shows the wage scales for the various jobs performed by workers in the silk mills. They were poorly paid for a five-and-a-half-day workweek compared to workers in other industries. (Courtesy of American Labor Museum/Botto House National Landmark.)

Paterson silk mill workers in one of the many smaller shops in the city and its surroundings are shown posing at their work site, surrounded by their machinery and tools, around 1910. (Courtesy of American Labor Museum/Botto House National Landmark.)

The silk industry provided work for many immigrants coming to this country in the late 19th and early 20th centuries. Manufacturers recruited skilled workers from silk centers in Europe. (Courtesy of American Labor Museum/Botto House National Landmark.)

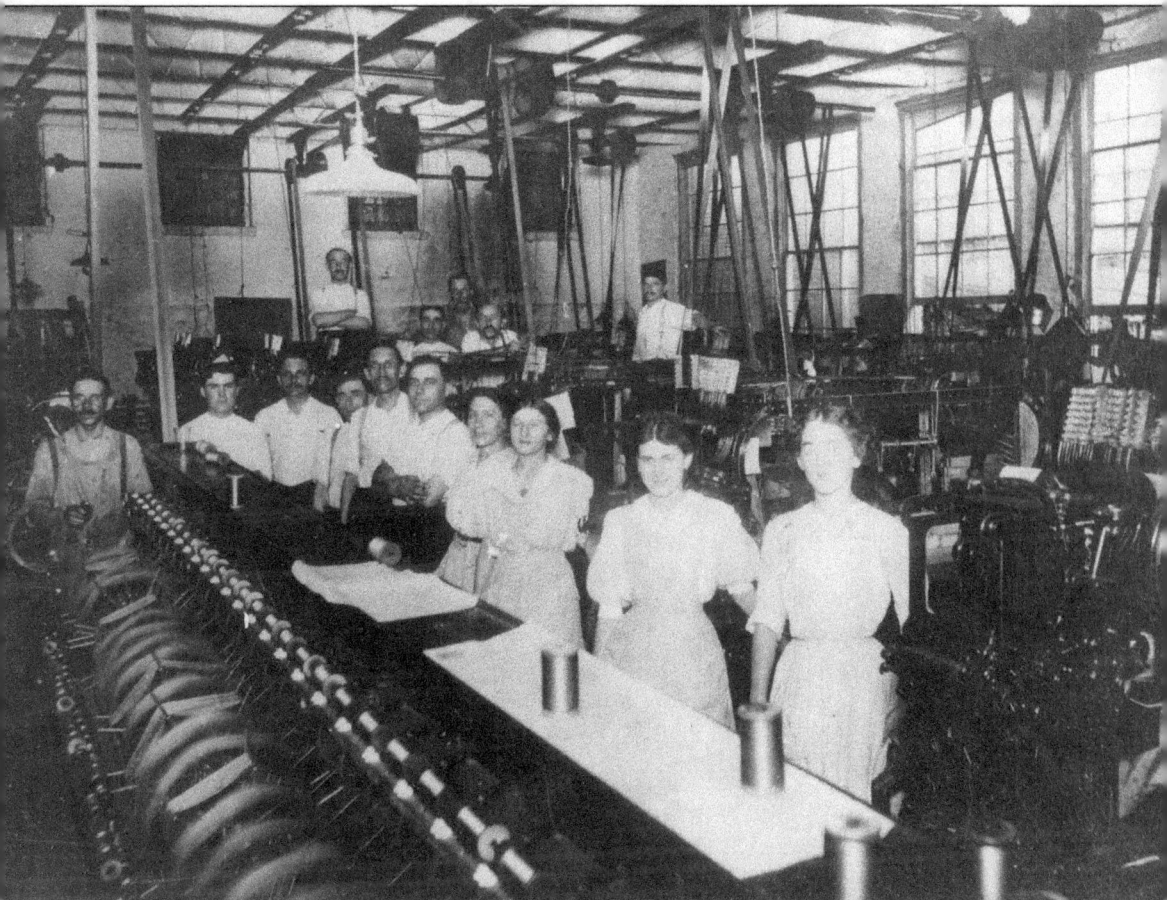

Men, women, and children worked at looms for long hours, often resulting in serious accidents and injuries. Women's unprotected hair would get caught in the machines, causing them to be scalped, and shoeless children were vulnerable to getting their feet caught in the machinery and losing toes. (Courtesy of American Labor Museum/Botto House National Landmark.)

New Jersey's laws required children to attend school until the age of 14 in the early 20th century. Many children, however, were forced to work in mills to help their families survive. There were workers who started in the mills as young as 8, 9, and 10 years old. These children grew to adulthood in the mills. (Courtesy of American Labor Museum/Botto House National Landmark.)

Three

THE SUBURB
OF HALEDON

Looking down the tree-lined Zabriskie Street in Haledon, Joffe's Drug Store sits on the left, opposite the Cedar Cliff Methodist Church. Located near Belmont Avenue, Haledon's main street, which carried the trolley car line, this drugstore and church were part of the hub of the borough. In 1891, electrified cars replaced horse-drawn trolleys on the tracks connecting the borough of Haledon with Paterson's industrial and commercial center. This efficient and fast form of transportation made it convenient for immigrants to acquire inexpensive land and homes in the suburbs and still have a means to travel to work. (Courtesy of American Labor Museum/Botto House National Landmark.)

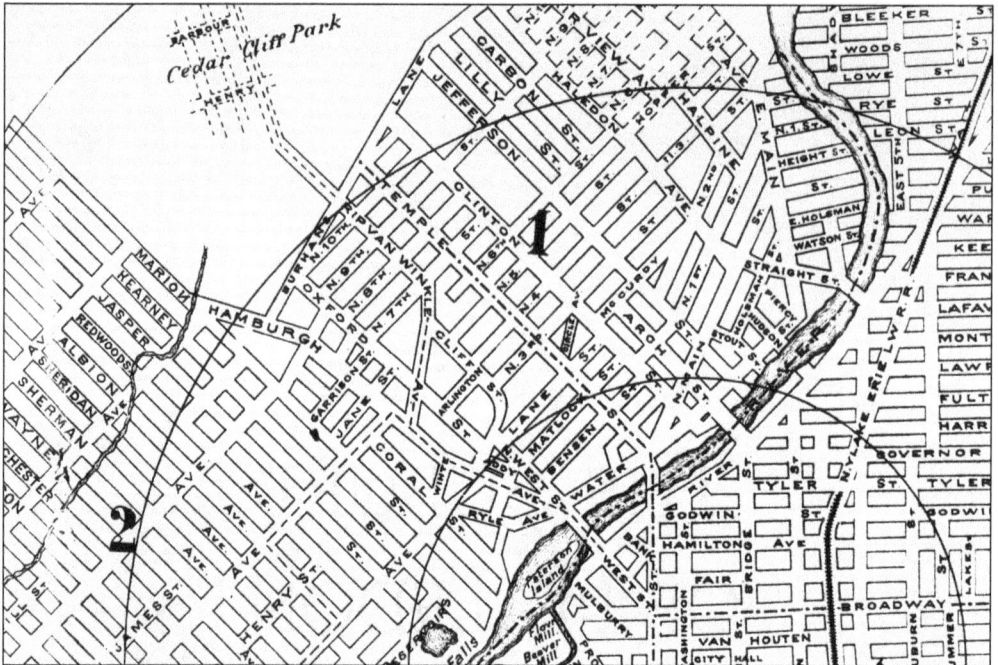

Cedar Cliff Park in Haledon was a place where immigrant families gathered on Sunday afternoons. Silk mills operated every weekday except Sunday. The little leisure time available to workers was frequently spent, weather permitting, in the outdoors with family and friends, far from the lint, oils, and fumes of the workplace. As the map indicates, the park was subject to development; Haledon's Barbour and Henry Streets, residential areas, were constructed there. (Courtesy of American Labor Museum/Botto House National Landmark.)

HOMES FOR WORKINGMEN!
🐖 THE DOREMUS FARM 🐖

On Red Woods Avenue, Jasper, Kearney, Marion & Doremus Streets, is now in the Market to be sold in City Lots.

FIFTY LOTS have been sold in the last three months without advertising, and without any special effort. About One Hundred Building Lots, some of the best on the whole tract, remain to be sold. RED WOODS AVENUE, twenty lots, from $150 up. JASPER STREET, twenty-five lots, from $125 up. KEARNEY STREET, five lots, $150 up. MARION STREET, four lots, $200 up. DOREMUS STREET, (running from Red Woods Avenue to Hamburgh Avenue), thirty-six lots, $200 up. All of these lots are well located, within five minutes walk of Hamburgh Avenue and the Union Avenue horse cars.

TERMS OF SALE TO SUIT BUYERS. $10 to $20 cash, balance in monthly instalments of $5 till paid. NO FORFEITURE OF PAYMENTS IN CASE OF SICKNESS OR BEING OUT OF WORK. A mortgage will be taken for two-thirds of the purchase money, payable in three years, with option to the buyer to pay it off sooner. TITLE GUARANTEED.

A PRINTED ABSTRACT OF TITLE furnished to every purchaser of a lot, showing the claim of Title for more than 200 years, from King Charles II to the Duke of York 1664, to Lord John Berkeley and Sir George Carteret 1665, to the Proprietors of East Jersey 1683, to George Willocks 1696, to Helmig Van Houten, Roel of Van Houten & Anthony Brockholst 1696, to Anthony Brockholst 1710, to Dominie David Marinus 1756, to Gerrit Van Houten 1760, to Ferris Ryerson 1816, to Ralph Doremus 1836, to the Doremus Land Improvement Company 1890.

Maps showing the location and price of Lots may be seen at the offices of the President and Treasurer,

Land promoters' advertisements encouraged working people and new immigrants to aspire to owning their own detached homes and gardens. Many sought to escape crowded city apartments and boardinghouses. Available lots near area trolley lines were attractive to working families. The laying of new track and the expansion of the trolley car lines relieved the congestion of urban centers. (Courtesy of Paterson Museum.)

68

The Cedar Cliff Land Company sought to offer reasonable real estate opportunities in Haledon to immigrant working families in the late 19th century. The fact that three silk mills were operating on the company's property and actively hired workers was an important incentive for workers to invest in a home of their own. (Courtesy of Paterson Museum.)

Working families with land in Haledon often had multifamily homes built so that their new houses generated rental income. Extra rooms were rented to boarders, or apartments were created and rented to help defray expenses. By the 1920s, practically every home was equipped with running water and electricity. (Courtesy of American Labor Museum/Botto House National Landmark.)

This aerial view of Haledon is a wintry scene of workers' homes across Hobart and Tilt Streets. From the size and style of the houses, it is clear that the area was not affluent, contrasting with the mansions and castle belonging to the silk barons in Paterson. (Courtesy of American Labor Museum/Botto House National Landmark.)

70

Signs were posted on empty lots throughout Haledon as a means of recruiting purchasers to buy and build a home. This vacant lot is on the corner of Tilt Street and Morrissee Avenue in Haledon. (Courtesy of American Labor Museum/Botto House National Landmark.)

The busy grocery market of the northern Italian Coda family prospered at its location along the trolley tracks of Belmont Avenue in Haledon. It catered to the Piedmontese community, offering home delivery of produce and goods via horse and wagon. (Courtesy of American Labor Museum/Botto House National Landmark.)

T&M Tavern stood on the corner of Henry and Van Dyke Streets in Haledon. Chuck Fredrichs is photographed tending bar. Haledon's taverns were frequented by workers. (Courtesy of American Labor Museum/Botto House National Landmark.)

Gaede's Pond was a favorite recreation spot for Haledon's immigrant families. The summer brought opportunities for fishing, boating, and picnicking, while ice-skating was popular in the winter. The pond was part of the Gaede estate, a country home located on the Newark Pompton Turnpike at the end of the trolley car line. The Gaede family hailed from Driesen, Germany, and headed the successful Gaede Silk Dyeing Company of Paterson, where many Haledon residents were employed. (Courtesy of American Labor Museum/Botto House National Landmark.)

Get Your Own Home.

WITH 50 or 100 Dollars you can get possession of a House and Lot, or One to Ten Acres of Land and a House.

This Property is situated at the foot of the Haledon Mountains, one mile from Paterson, at the terminus of the electric car line which connects it with Paterson.

THE GROUND IS HIGH,

   THE ATMOSPHERE IS INVIGORATING,

    HEALTH PRODUCING

      AND HEALTH PRESERVING.

I own over 400 Acres of Land; understand well I am not Agent, I sell only my own Land with a clear title.

If you wont to GET YOUR OWN HOME, see first,

Yours truly,

WM. BUSCHMANN,
HALEDON, N. J.

William Buschmann was a leading citizen in Haledon who also ran a resort, beer garden, and brewery. He is featured in a real estate advertisement in the Paterson Directory of 1912–1913. (Courtesy of American Labor Museum/Botto House National Landmark.)

An advertisement in the *Paterson Morning Call* in 1890 promoted land sales in the borough of Haledon to immigrants and working families. "Get a slice of the Earth," was the land promoters' slogan. It attracted upwardly mobile workers, who were eager to leave crowded city dwellings and were able to afford the inexpensive, city-sized lots of 25 by 100 feet along the trolley tracks. Newer ethnic groups, including the northern Italians and Syrians, added to the older Scotch, English, and Colonial Dutch stock of Haledon. (Courtesy of American Labor Museum/Botto House National Landmark.)

The Whittaker children of Haledon pose in their "Sunday finest," clothing worn on special occasions. (Courtesy of American Labor Museum/Botto House National Landmark.)

Great-grandfather Stansfield of Haledon sits in his garden, surrounded by flowers, holding his cane. (Courtesy of American Labor Museum/Botto House National Landmark.)

Department of Public Education,

Township of Manchester, Passaic County, N. J.

This is to Certify that

_____

a pupil of Public School No. Two,

... Grammar Grade, ...

_____ year, having completed the course of study prescribed for this department, and having passed the required examination, is hereby entitled to promotion.

_____ Teacher.

_____ Principal.

In concurrence with the foregoing, the **Board of Education** *has granted this Certificate, this _____ day of _____ A. D., _____*

_____ President.

_____ District Clerk.

NEW JERSEY

This certificate was awarded to student Ruth Heill for completing seven years of grammar school at Public School No. 2 in 1906. When Haledon later became a borough in 1908, it was called the Kossuth Street School. (Courtesy of American Labor Museum/Botto House National Landmark.)

Home sites were on small lots. The house was small and cramped. Backyards were adjacent, so people knew their neighbors. Gardens were planted so that the family had fresh vegetables for the summer months and then canned them for use in the winter. Many working families raised their own poultry. On small lots, they could be quite self-sufficient. (Courtesy of American Labor Museum/Botto House National Landmark.)

Real Estate and Insurance.

Established 1868.

James A. Morrisse

INCORPORATED.

MORRISSE BLDG., 314 Main, Cor. Ward St.

REAL ESTATE,

Insurance and Steamship Agency.

Fire, Plate Glass, Employers' Liability, Steam Boiler, Teams, Burglary, Accident an
Health Insurance.   Surety and Fidelity Bonds.   Money to Loan on Bond and Mortga

STEAMSHIP TICKETS FOR ALL THE TRANS-ATLANTIC LINES.

James A. Morrissee was a banker, broker, and vice president of Electric Railway Company, based in Paterson. A street in Haledon is named in his honor. (Courtesy of American Labor Museum/ Botto House National Landmark.)

The Silk City Band was a marching band that participated in town parades and other community events. Business or organizational sponsors afforded the musicians the opportunity to purchase uniforms and instruments. (Courtesy of American Labor Museum/Botto House National Landmark.)

Pietro and Maria Botto stand on the porch of their newly constructed house on the corner of Norwood Street and Mason Avenue in Haledon around 1913. They are accompanied by their neighbors, the Frignoca and Coda families. (Courtesy of American Labor Museum/Botto House National Landmark.)

After 15 years of weaving in textile mills, Pietro and Maria saved and borrowed enough money to purchase land and build a home of their own in the borough of Haledon. Newly built in this photograph of 1908, the concrete-block and clapboard home of the Bottos was of a housing type termed a tenement dwelling because rooms ran off a central hall, which had the potential of being divided into four apartments or further into rooms to be let. The Bottos always retained the first floor for family use and rented two three-room units on the second floor. (Courtesy of American Labor Museum/Botto House National Landmark.)

This photograph of Elizabeth Roe, which is printed on a postcard, is a typical means of communication between families. A note would be written on the reverse side for the recipient to learn of any news. (Courtesy of American Labor Museum/Botto House National Landmark.)

Professional photographers were paid to take photographs of family members. The images were printed on postcards and mailed to relatives. (Courtesy of American Labor Museum/Botto House National Landmark.)

High School

AMELIA BERRY BERDAN
MARY MEAD BERDAN
||SARAH HELEN BRIDGE
FLORENCE EDNA COLOMBO

BLANCHE ANNA ROAT
LILLEOUS ROE
ELLA MAUDE SIMONDS
*FRED JOHN ULRICH

Eighth Grade

Samuel Abraham
Julia Lauretta Boothney
Fridolina Gertrude Botz
Anna Mary Birgels
Barbara C. Ellis
Charles W. Ellis
William Ford
Robert H. Gaede
Edwin Augustus Leonhard

Albert J. Loetscher
Robert F. McKersie
*Elizabeth Hannah Roe
Edward T. Robinson
Bruno J. Rochelle
||Katharine Schoonmaker
Wainwright D. Twing
Emily Sevilla Van Hovenberg
Alice Ethel Van Hovenberg

*First honor.
||Second honor.

The Piano used on this occasion is from the warerooms of L. and M. Kirsinger, Broadway and Church Streets, Paterson.

Combined Commencement

Exercises

of the

High and Grammar

Schools

of

Manchester Township, Passaic County,

New Jersey.

School Number Two, Haledon

June the Twenty-first

Nineteen Hundred and Six.

This program is for the combined commencement ceremonies of the elementary and secondary schools of Haledon, around 1906. There were only 8 high school and 18 grammar school graduates because so many children worked in the mills. (Courtesy of American Labor Museum/ Botto House National Landmark.)

LIFE MEMBERSHIP CARD

We hereby certify that

Kittie H. Roe

has been enrolled as a Life Member of

Star of Bethlehem Chapter, No. 17, O. E. S.

Date *Nov. 18, 1936*

Helen Blyth
W. MATRON

Kittie H. Roe
SECRETARY

Joseph Grimshaw
W. PATRON

Social, ethnic, and religious organizations were formed by groups in small communities to bring together people for various purposes. This life membership card is for Elizabeth H. "Kittie" Roe, secretary of the Star of Bethlehem Chapter No. 17, Order of the Eastern Star. (Courtesy of American Labor Museum/Botto House National Landmark.)

New Jersey State Board of Education

NORMAL SCHOOL CERTIFICATE

ELEMENTARY

THIS CERTIFIES THAT *Elizabeth Hannah Roe*

IS A GRADUATE OF THE NEW JERSEY STATE NORMAL SCHOOL AT MONTCLAIR,

General

COURSE, AND IS LICENSED TO TEACH IN ANY ELEMENTARY SCHOOL; TO SUPERVISE TEACHING IN ANY ELEMENTARY BRANCH OF STUDY; TO SUPERVISE ANY ELEMENTARY DEPARTMENT; TO BE THE PRINCIPAL OF ANY ELEMENTARY SCHOOL THAT IS UNDER A CITY SUPERINTENDENT; TO BE THE PRINCIPAL OF AN ELEMENTARY SCHOOL OR THE ELEMENTARY SCHOOLS OF A DISTRICT EMPLOYING NOT MORE THAN NINE ASSISTANT TEACHERS AND NOT UNDER A LOCAL SUPERINTENDENT OR SUPERVISING PRINCIPAL, FOR THE TERM OF TEN YEARS.

THIS CERTIFICATE MAY BE MADE PERMANENT AFTER TWO YEARS OF SUCCESSFUL EXPERIENCE IN TEACHING.

DONE AT THE CITY OF TRENTON THIS *8th* DAY OF *Jan.* 19*13*

C. N. Kendall

STATE COMMISSIONER OF EDUCATION.

Charles S. Chapin

PRINCIPAL OF THE STATE NORMAL SCHOOL AT MONTCLAIR.

John Calvin Roe lived at 35 Zabriskie Street in Haledon. Roe Street was later named in his honor. This normal school certificate, dated June 8, 1913, entitles his descendant Elizabeth Hannah Roe be a teacher and administrator in elementary schools. (Courtesy of American Labor Museum/Botto House National Landmark.)

A normal school was a two-year college attended by students (predominantly women) who studied to become teaching professionals in the school systems. Haledon resident Elizabeth Hannah Roe is pictured with the graduating class of 1913. (Courtesy of American Labor Museum/Botto House National Landmark.)

Roe proudly poses for a photograph holding her diploma on her graduation day in 1913. (Courtesy of American Labor Museum/Botto House National Landmark.)

Roe, a Haledon resident, is pictured with her first-grade class in the year 1893. She later went on to become a New York City schoolteacher. (Courtesy of American Labor Museum/Botto House National Landmark.)

St. Mary's Parish House, Haledon, N. J.

This scene of the snow-covered street is in the foreground of St. Mary's Parish House in Haledon. It was built in 1889. (Courtesy of American Labor Museum/Botto House National Landmark.)

Four

COMMUNITY LIFE

FESTA TRIVERESE
PRO PATRONATO SCOLASTICO
PATERSON N. J. SEP. 3RD 1921.

PHOTO BY
C. DIXTZ.

The Alpine Club was composed of immigrants from the Piedmont section of Italy and their families. In this photograph taken in 1921, members gather next to the club's hall (at far right) located at the corner of John and Geyer Streets in Haledon. Battista Doda (first row, third from right and wearing a vest), a weaver who arrived in the United States from Valle Mosso in 1905 and settled in the Haledon area with his wife, Olimpia, who was also a weaver, was typical of the Alpine Club's membership in terms of occupation and support of this fraternal and charitable organization. (Courtesy of Doris Roffino Ververs.)

SAAL BROS.,
SCHUETZEN PARK,

SAAL BROS., Proprietors,

PATERSON, N. J.

TELEPHONE CALL 499.

Arrangements for Pic-Nics, Summer-Night Festivals, Target Excursions, etc., can be made at the "CASTLE," Schuetzen Park, or 65 Broadway.

Haledon Electric Cars Direct to the Park.

Schuetzen Park was a destination for Sunday outings for many Haledon residents. It was accessible via an electric trolley car line. Haledon residents could get away from their labor-filled lives for a little while. Schuetzen Park provided picnic grounds, ample space for festivals, and rides for children. (Courtesy of American Labor Museum/Botto House National Landmark.)

When Haledon residents would prefer a much simpler and affordable Sunday outing, they would go to Indian Rock in their own hometown. Haledon families would bring a picnic lunch and enjoy a good time with family and friends. (Courtesy of American Labor Museum/Botto House National Landmark.)

In Haledon, Guild Hall was a meeting place and social hall for the Frisan Society. West Friesland in the Netherlands, a heavily agricultural area, was the homeland of many immigrants who took up dye house work in and around Paterson. Among the Hollanders, Harry Hagerdon assumed a leadership role during the 1913 Paterson silk strike and spoke frequently at Paterson and Haledon strikers' meetings. (Courtesy of American Labor Museum/Botto House National Landmark.)

In 1928, the northern Italian immigrants from the Piedmont region organized their first annual outing in Paterson. Many Haledon families were in attendance. (Courtesy of American Labor

PIEMONTESI CLUBS
JLY 1928

REID STUD
61 B'WAY
PATERSON

Museum/Botto House National Landmark.)

This 1900 German men's glee club was called the Haledon Eintracht. (Courtesy of American Labor Museum/Botto House National Landmark.)

Immigrants who came from the same country of origin organized cultural and social groups. This German club gathered in Haledon for a Sunday outing. (Courtesy of American Labor Museum/Botto House National Landmark.)

Taken on October 2, 1927, this photograph is of the members of the St. Michael's Association. Immigrants who professed the same faith would join their church or temple synagogue and organize associations to help raise funds for their place of worship. (Courtesy of American Labor Museum/Botto House National Landmark.)

The Ideal Music Club in Haledon created this mourning photograph in remembrance of and respect to Pietro Coda, who was a member of the group. The bottom of the picture reads "for the lost partner" in Italian. (Courtesy of American Labor Museum/Botto House National Landmark.)

The Ideal Music Club of Haledon minted coins bearing its insignia and name as a membership souvenir for its members. (Courtesy of American Labor Museum/Botto House National Landmark.)

This is a collage of photographs of the officers and members of the Ideal Music Club of Haledon during the years 1901–1907. The members met in one another's homes for dancing and singing and entertaining families and friends. They also played at weddings in the community. (Courtesy of American Labor Museum/Botto House National Landmark.)

Members of the Bocchio family strum their string instruments for this family portrait. Music was an integral part of many immigrant households. (Courtesy of American Labor Museum/Botto House National Landmark.)

The invention of the affordable automobile enabled families to travel outside their immediate surroundings for an outing. These Piedmontese men, women, and children proudly pose with their new means of transportation. (Courtesy of American Labor Museum/Botto House National Landmark.)

Albina

Adele

Eva

Olga

The daughters of Maria and Pietro Botto, immigrants from northern Italy, lived in apartments in their parents' home in Haledon when they married and began raising families. The daughters worked in area silk mills and added their income to the household. After the silk strike of 1913, a Botto daughter kept her name a secret when seeking employment, as she feared the reprisals of the manufacturers against strikers. (Courtesy of American Labor Museum/Botto House National Landmark.)

St John's Parish Church Choir
Conversazione
DANCE PROGRAMME

1. Waltz	Songs
2. Quadrille	11. Quadrille
3. Polka	12. Waltz
4. Lancers	13. Scotch Reel
Songs	Coffee
5. Waltz	14. Lancers
6. Highland Schottische	15. Polka
Tea	16. Waltz
7. Quadrille	17. Quadrille
8. Polka	Songs
9. Lancers	18. Lancers
10. Waltz	19. Quadrille
20. Waltz	

St. John's Parish Church was the backbone of the Irish community in Paterson's Dublin neighborhood. This program for a dance was lettered by Thomas Barr, a jacquard silk designer, as a donation. (Courtesy of American Labor Museum/Botto House National Landmark.)

Churches helped to acclimate the immigrants to American life. St. Paul's Lutheran Church supported its own parochial school, where lessons were conducted in German as well as English. Many of the children left school after receiving the sacrament of confirmation to work in the mills. (Courtesy of American Labor Museum/Botto House National Landmark.)

Many members of the ladies guild of St. Paul's Lutheran Church were of German and Swiss descent. These women worked in the mills and were famed for their warping and ribbon-weaving skills. Being a part of the church group helped them to preserve their language and Old World customs. (Courtesy of American Labor Museum/Botto House National Landmark.)

The sport of cricket was introduced from England. There were several good cricket fields in and around the city of Paterson. The Paterson Cricket Club's field was prominent. This field was located in Haledon near the corner of Belmont Avenue and King Street and was part of what was known as Cedar Cliff Park. (Courtesy of American Labor Museum/Botto House National Landmark.)

Swiss and German workers organized athletic clubs called Turn Vereins. Pictured above is an instructor with a young women's gymnastic society. (Courtesy of American Labor Museum/Botto House National Landmark.)

This men's Arbeiter Turn Verein photograph was taken in 1906 and contains portraits of German workers who belonged to the society at that time. (Courtesy of American Labor Museum/Botto House National Landmark.)

Published and distributed under permit number 55 authorized by the Act of October 6 1917 on file t the Post Office at New York by order of the President, A. S. BURLESON Postmaster General.

ANNO IV. No. 22   L'ORDINE DEI FIGLI D'ITALIA IN AMERICA HA 852 LOGGE   NEW YORK 1 GIUGNO

ORDINE FIGLI D'ITALIA

LIBERTÀ · UGUAGLIANZA
O.F.D'I.
IN A.
FRATELLANZA
IN AMERICA

Bollettino   Ufficiale

SI PUBBLICA IL SABATO

Entered as second-class matter July 1st 1916, at the Post Office at New York, N. Y., under the act of March 3, 1879.

Published weekly by Supreme Executive Board of Ordine Figli d'Italia in America — Subscription price: 1 dollar a year — 1 copy 5 cent

Direzione ed Amministrazione: 226 LAFAYETTE STREET, NEEW YORK CITY — Telephone: Spring 563

Nel giorno sacro alla glorificazione dell' Italia negli Stati Uniti

Sons of Italy was an Italian newspaper published in New York City. It was read by most Italians in Haledon and Paterson. Newspapers such as this one made Italians feel a little more at home, and they could also keep up with their Italian heritage. (Courtesy of American Labor Museum/Botto House National Landmark.)

This group of Italian immigrants from the Fiesta Foratellaze Italiana poses for their organizational photograph in September 1920. (Courtesy of American Labor Museum/Botto House National Landmark.)

Piedmontese neighbors from Haledon enjoy a day's outing to Steeplechase Park, Rockaway Beach, New York, around 1930. (Courtesy of American Labor Museum/Botto House National Landmark.)

Immigrant children were able to socialize with each other at church. Picnics helped to foster a good relationship between children of different nationalities. St. Mary's Church was incorporated on August 26, 1899. It was known as the "Oldham Mission," one of the oldest churches in Passaic County. The church is widely known for its annual dinner and bazaar held every December. (Courtesy of American Labor Museum/Botto House National Landmark.)

On a Sunday outing, family and friends of Haledon's Piedmontese families gather for a photograph in a wooded area at the end of the trolley car line. (Courtesy of Laura Van De Voort Allaghi.)

Haledon residents gather at the Eagle Rock area in 1924 for relaxation. (Courtesy of Laura Van De Voort Allaghi.)

Haledon had many men and women who served during World War I. Upon their return, a parade was held in their honor on September 13, 1919. Haledon officials, organizations, children, and the veterans all marched collectively through Haledon. Afterward a banquet was held with

entertainment by professionals from New York City, followed by dancing. All the veterans were presented with medals to commemorate their service to their country. (Courtesy of American Labor Museum/Botto House National Landmark.)

In this photograph, Haledon musicians are gathering for an important rehearsal of their musical arrangements. (Courtesy of American Labor Museum/Botto House National Landmark.)

Members of the Highlander Association are dressed in their full regalia of Scottish origin. (Courtesy of American Labor Museum/Botto House National Landmark.)

Pictured here are members of the Uthmann Mannerchor, established in Haledon in 1913. (Courtesy of American Labor Museum/Botto House National Landmark.)

Turn Halle Concordia Brass Band is posing in front of Turn Halle Beer Tunnel. (Courtesy of American Labor Museum/Botto House National Landmark.)

Here is a stock certificate for one share of the Co-Operative Butcher Shop, printed at $5 a share, dated September 22, 1917. (Courtesy of American Labor Museum/Botto House National Landmark.)

Five

LABOR ACTIVISM

This program cover is from the pageant performed by the 1913 Paterson silk strikers at Madison Square Garden in New York City. The cover was designed by Robert Edmund Jones. (Courtesy of the American Labor Museum/Botto House National Landmark.)

All union members carried their membership cards as another form of identification. Alessandro Picchetto was a silk worker and a member of the IWW. He and his fellow Wobblies paid their union dues in person on a monthly basis and received a stamp in their membership book as a receipt of payment. (Courtesy of American Labor Museum/ Botto House National Landmark.)

The handshake represents the brotherhood of union members, whose motto is "In Union is Strength." (Courtesy of American Labor Museum/Botto House National Landmark.)

Striking silk mill workers parade through Paterson in 1913, displaying American flags and placards reading, "We are on Strike for Bread and Butter!" The unity of the broad-silk weavers, dyers' helpers, and ribbon weavers was unprecedented during the general strike that began on February 25, 1913. (Courtesy of American Labor Museum/Botto House National Landmark.)

The O'Brien Detective Agency of Newark was hired to protect the scabs, workers who did not honor the strike and crossed picket lines to enter the mills, during the 1913 Paterson silk strike. (Courtesy of American Labor Museum/Botto House National Landmark.)

Silk mill workers who picketed the mills were jailed for disorderly conduct, which very often was a result of simply calling a strikebreaker a scab. When arrested, they would go to jail singing "The Internationale." (Courtesy of American Labor Museum/Botto House National Landmark.)

Paterson police chief John Bimson ordered his force to padlock Turn Halle, the place where the strikers assembled. It was a way to prevent the strikers from meeting with the IWW leaders and prolonging the strike. (Courtesy of American Labor Museum/Botto House National Landmark.)

Carlo Tresca, a labor leader from the IWW, spoke at the union meetings held at the Botto House in Haledon during the 1913 Paterson silk strike. (Courtesy of American Labor Museum/Botto House National Landmark.)

CARLO TRESCA I.W.W. SPEAKER
1913.
PATERSON, N.J.

At a strike meeting in Haledon, speakers address the crowd of over 20,000 from the second-floor balcony of the Botto House, located at 83 Norwood Street. (Courtesy of American Labor Museum/ Botto House National Landmark.)

As many as 20,000 striking silk mill workers representing nine ethnic groups gathered in Haledon at the house of Maria and Pietro Botto, northern Italian silk workers, during the Paterson silk strike of 1913. Haledon mayor William Brueckmann guaranteed the safety of the workers. The hills surrounding the Bottos' home formed a natural amphitheater for out-of-town speakers from the IWW, who addressed the crowds from the house's second-floor balcony. (Courtesy of American Labor Museum/Botto House National Landmark.)

This photograph was taken from the Botto House as the thousands of Paterson silk mill strikers assembled outside. The Cerrutti family's background home provided a front porch for better viewing. (Courtesy of American Labor Museum/Botto House National Landmark.)

Considered a hero to workers during the 1913 Paterson silk strike, Haledon mayor William Brueckmann, elected on the Socialist ticket, allowed nearly 25,000 workers to peacefully assemble in the town without government interference. (Courtesy of American Labor Museum/Botto House National Landmark.)

Strike organizers arranged for groups of children to be temporarily adopted by families sympathetic to the strikers' cause. Without a large strike fund, workers were forced to dip into savings, ask for credit at local grocery stores, or place their children in homes outside of Paterson in order to keep them fed and clothed. Children of Jewish strikers pose for a group portrait prior to being evacuated from the city during the strike. (Courtesy of American Labor Museum/Botto House National Landmark.)

In mid-February 1913, leaders of the IWW, called the Wobblies, came to Paterson to give voice to the strike. The labor leaders, from left to right, are Patrick Quinlan, Carlo Tresca, Elizabeth Gurley Flynn, Adolf Lessic, and "Big Bill" Haywood. (Courtesy of American Labor Museum/ Botto House National Landmark.)

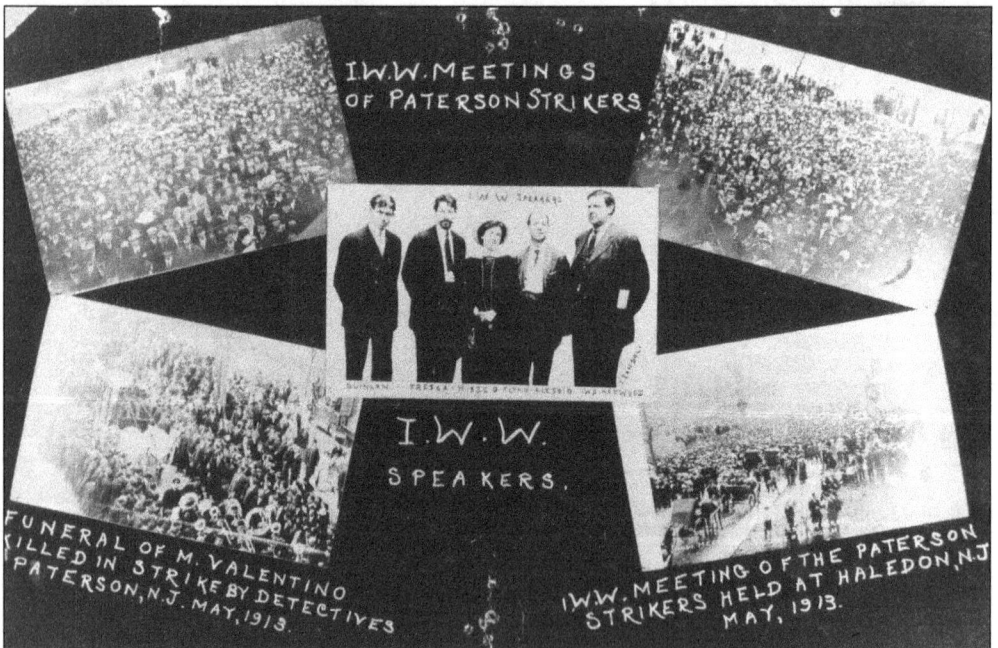

Here is a collage of photographs representing the events surrounding the 1913 Paterson silk strike. (Courtesy of American Labor Museum/Botto House National Landmark.)

Caroline Gold (holding guitar) took part in the 1913 strike. Seen here with the sister that she raised and a favorite cousin, Gold went into the Paterson mills as a teenager and played an active part in the 1913 strike. At Sunday rallies in front of historic Botto House, she sang with the chorus up on the second-floor balcony, leading the thousands of assembled strikers in labor songs. (Courtesy of American Labor Museum/Botto House National Landmark.)

During the Paterson silk strike of 1913, songs were sung by the strikers to raise their morale. These songs were meaningful and helped keep the striking workers united. (Courtesy of American Labor Museum/Botto House National Landmark.)

FOR THE STRIKE IN PATERSON

Mel. *Der Papst lebt herrlich in der Welt.*

1. Take off your Clogs, be very quiet,
   And leave the box, we'll go on strike;
   So said the Workers, when they left
   The Silk Dye House, with all its Graft.

2. The Broad Silk Weavers left the Loom
   The Ribbon Weavers followed soon;
   For better wages they asked too,
   Instead of four Looms they want two.

3. For the glorious Eight Hour Day
   Out on the strike we all will stay,
   Until the Bosses will give in,
   And then, the Victory we'll win.

4. But if you go and play the Scab
   Some day you will not be so glad,
   Because the Union then will say
   That out the Shop you'll have to stay.

5. Now take my word, I wont say much,
   If Yankee, German or if Dutch,
   If Belgian, Polish or from Italy,
   The victory will ours be.

6. Be good and stay with us together
   And do not mind the weary weather;
   Make ready Kettle, Knife and Fork,
   Because we all go soon to work.

Paterson, N. J. the 15th day of Febr. 1913.
W. F. D.

THE NEW ERA PRESS 26 PROSPECT STREET

119

Striking silk workers and their families form the funeral procession of Valentino Modestino as it moves through Paterson from the Catholic church on East Nineteenth Street to the Laurel Grove Cemetery. (Courtesy of American Labor Museum/Botto House National Landmark.)

Employed in a local file works, Modestino returned on April 17, 1913, to his home in the Riverside section of Paterson, where he witnessed one of many confrontations between striking dyers' helpers and O'Brien detectives. Detectives fired several shots to intimidate the crowds; a bullet struck Modestino in the back as he stood on the front stoop of his home. He died three days after the shooting. The silk manufacturers exercised control over the police of Paterson, and the detective who shot Modestino was not indicted. (Courtesy of American Labor Museum/Botto House National Landmark.)

This photograph shows a procession of men, women, and children at the funeral of Modestino. Modestino, an innocent bystander, was killed by a detective's stray bullet during the 1913 Paterson silk strike. (Courtesy of American Labor Museum/Botto House National Landmark.)

Thousands gathered to pay tribute to Modestino, an innocent bystander who was accidentally killed by a detective's stray bullet during the 1913 Paterson silk strike. (Courtesy of American Labor Museum/Botto House National Landmark.)

On April 17, 1913, at 6:30 p.m., Valentino Modestino was shot while standing on the front stoop of his home holding his baby daughter, Josephine. O'Brien detectives who were guarding the Weidmann Plant fired shots to intimidate the crowd. Modestino was hit in the back. Modestino died three days later at Paterson General Hospital. (Courtesy of American Labor Museum/Botto House National Landmark.)

At the end of June 1913, Vincenzo Madonna, a broad-silk weaver, was fatally wounded in a scuffle with strikebreakers. (Courtesy of American Labor Museum/Botto House National Landmark.)

Seen here are IWW leader Elizabeth Gurley Flynn on the right, Eva Botto standing, and a friend of Eva on the left at the Botto House, in front of the grape arbor in Haledon. (Courtesy of American Labor Museum/Botto House National Landmark.)

N? 241

$5.00

This is to certify that Mr. *M. Baok*

is a member of the

Hebrew Labor Lyceum Associati

$5.00

# of Paterson, N. J.

Aug 24 191 8

J. Miller _____ **President**

H. Heller _____ **Secretary**

Grossman Print 39 West Street

The Hebrew Labor Lyceum was the meeting place for the Workmen's Circle, or Arbeiter Ring, a national Jewish fraternal organization steeped in the socialist tradition of supporting civil rights, trade unions, and active participation in many political and social causes. The Hebrew Labor Lyceum was the site of concerts, lectures, and political discussions. (Courtesy of American Labor Museum/Botto House National Landmark.)

IL LAVORATORE DELLA SETA

DEVOTO ALL' INTERESSE DI TUTTI I LAVORATORI — SPECIALMENTE AI LAVORATORI DELLA SETA

VOLUME I., No. 1.	PATERSON, N. J.	3 NOVEMBER, 1917 PREZZO, 2c.

LO SAPETE VOI?

Che fino dal 25 Settembre, circa tre mila tessitori, sono in isciopero? Che lo sciopero involve circa sessanta fabbriche di Broad Silk? Sapete voi di che cosa si tratta? Voi non

LE OTTO ORE DI LAVORO

Molto se n'e scritto e molto se ne parlato. Tutti e tutte le vogliono. Come averle? Bisogna domandarle. Sta bene, ma le concederanno i pad-

tazioni ci quadagna questa o quella organizzazione, questa o quella uni- one. Noi desideriamo, che siccome le Nove Ore l'hanno auto tutti i lavo-

LA MAIN SILK CO.

Fino dal 3 Ott. questa fabbrica e insciopero. Il motivo è stato che il pardone si rifiuto di riconoscere il vecchio comitato. I lavoratori, maggioranza italiani, visto che si

Many immigrant groups printed their own newspapers in their native language. The translation on this 1917 Italian newspaper is "the silk worker." (Courtesy of American Labor Museum/Botto House National Landmark.)

A large population of immigrants from Europe belonged to the Socialist Party in the United States. This is a membership book of the Italian Socialist Federation. Haledon mayor William Brueckmann was elected on the Socialist Party ticket in 1912. (Courtesy of American Labor Museum/Botto House National Landmark.)

126

Labor Day was a true workers' holiday, on which parades and picnics were organized. This photograph of the uniformed members of the Butchers' Union Local 454 demonstrates the solidarity of the workers who assembled on Labor Day, September 6, 1915. (Courtesy of American Labor Museum/Botto House National Landmark.)

This certificate of the Labor Cooperative National Bank of Paterson was issued to Abram Muse of Haledon in 1924. The immigrants of Paterson and Haledon joined ethnic and worker associations, including financial cooperatives. Many cooperative agencies reflected the political radicalism of the workers. (Courtesy of American Labor Museum/Botto House National Landmark.)

ACROSS AMERICA, PEOPLE ARE DISCOVERING SOMETHING WONDERFUL. THEIR HERITAGE.

Arcadia Publishing is the leading local history publisher in the United States. With more than 3,000 titles in print and hundreds of new titles released every year, Arcadia has extensive specialized experience chronicling the history of communities and celebrating America's hidden stories, bringing to life the people, places, and events from the past. To discover the history of other communities across the nation, please visit:

www.arcadiapublishing.com

Customized search tools allow you to find regional history books about the town where you grew up, the cities where your friends and family live, the town where your parents met, or even that retirement spot you've been dreaming about.

MAP SEARCH